OWLS
Whoo are they?

Kila Jarvis and **Denver W. Holt**

Illustrated by Leslie Leroux and Courtney Couch

"Owlphabet" letters by Ed Jenne

IN COOPERATION WITH THE OWL RESEARCH INSTITUTE

1996
Mountain Press Publishing Company
Missoula, Montana

Third Printing, May 2000

Illustrations on pages 1, 3, 5, 7, 9, 11, 13, 15, 17, 19, 21, 23,
29, 31, 35, 37, 41, 43, 47, 51, and 53 © 1996 Leslie Leroux

Cover illustration and illustrations on pages 25, 27,
33, 39, 45, 49, and 55 © 1996 Courtney Couch

Illustrated capital letters © 1996 Ed Jenne

Book design by Kim Ericsson

The Owl Research Institute is a nonprofit organization that studies
the biology and ecology of owls and shares its findings with the public
and the scientific community. For more information contact the
Owl Research Institute, P. O. Box 8335, Missoula, MT 59807.

PRINTED IN HONG KONG BY MANTEC PRODUCTION COMPANY

Library of Congress Cataloging-in-Publication Data

Jarvis, Kila, 1965–
    Owls : whoo are they? / Kila Jarvis and Denver W. Holt.
        p. cm.
    Includes bibliographical references (p.   ) and index.
    Summary: Explores the biology, amazing adaptations, and natural history of these birds of prey
which are silent-winged creatures of the night.
    ISBN 0-87842-336-2 (paper : alk. paper)
    1. Owls—Juvenile literature. [1. Owls.] I. Holt, D. W. (Denver W.) II. Title.
QL696.S8J36   1996
598.9'7—dc20   96-3174
                                                                          CIP
                                                                          AC

Mountain Press Publishing Company
P. O. Box 2399 • Missoula, MT 59806
406-728-1900 • 800-234-5308

To Amanda, Ben, Nick, Britney, my family, and my students—
for your love of owls and support of me.
—K. J.

To my nephew and niece, Jonhenry and Justine—
so you may get an early start appreciating wildlife and conservation.
—D. W. H.

Praise for
OWLS *Whoo are they?*

"A wonderfully user-friendly book that presents a vast amount of information. . . . Anyone not familiar with these magnificent raptors, and those who are already fans of owls, will thoroughly enjoy this educational and delightful book."

—School Library Journal

"Every page brings to light good stuff. Adult readers will learn as much as the kids with this lovely and informative book."

—Boston Globe

"Kids age 8 and older will find this a fine attention grabber, with large paragraph headings introducing lively subjects."

—Children's Bookwatch

"This look at owls is as good as it gets for a children's nature book."

—The (Everett, Wash.) Herald

"Fascinating and mysterious, owls are important predators that help keep ecosystems in balance. This delightful fact-filled book lets us explore the wonderful world of owls and *whoo* they really are."

—Gary M. Stolz, Chief Naturalist
U.S. Fish & Wildlife Service

A delightfully versatile book with superb illustrations that may be used by eight year olds as well as adults. The elegance of the format makes the information readily available to busy teachers and learners at all levels. . . . a nice addition to teacher collections and school libraries. . . . a nice gift for an elementary student. I heartily recommend the book to anyone interested in learning more about owls."

—Linda L. Robinson
Montana Science Teachers Association

"Well written and biologically correct. . . . the most up-to-date, comprehensive, and fair discussion of these magnificent aerial predators that I've seen. OWLS *Whoo are they?* . . . should be a standard reference for every school library in the country."

—Bob Hernbrode, Wildlife Manager VI
Colorado Watchable Wildlife, Colorado Division of Wildlife

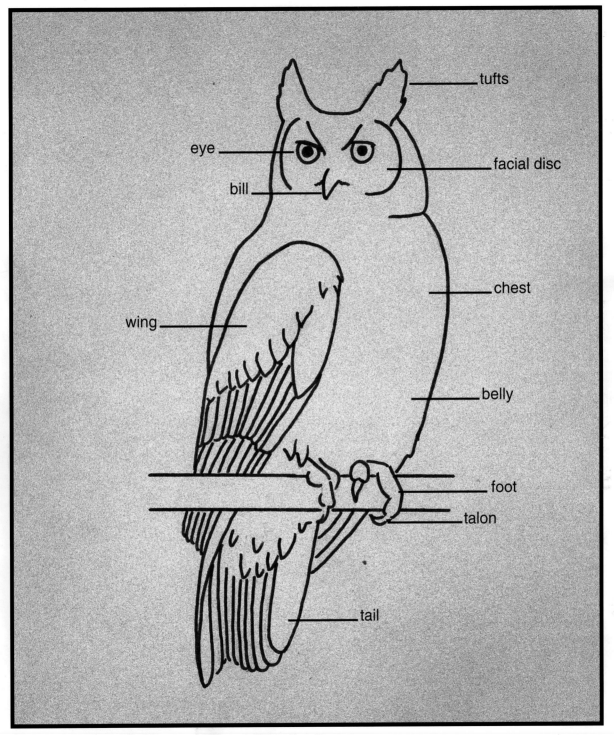

tufts

eye

facial disc

bill

chest

wing

belly

foot

talon

tail

Owl identification

Whoo . . . do you know that has eyes as big as yours, loves to stay up late, but would choose a mouse over pizza for lunch? A Great Horned Owl? Maybe a Barred Owl? Either of these birds fits that description—along with many other species of owls. Read on and explore the amazing adaptations and natural history of these silent-winged creatures of the night.

Great Horned Owl

wls Are Ancient

Bones and other remains of ancient animal life, called **fossils,** tell us that owls have lived on earth for 55 million years. So, owls have been around more than a million times longer than you have.

If you studied ancient cave paintings, tools, artwork, and legends, you would discover that owls have fascinated people for thousands of years. In some cultures, people thought owls were symbols of life and good health. In other cultures, people thought owls brought bad luck or even death.

The European Little Owl was sacred to Athena, the goddess of wisdom who was worshiped by the Greeks in ancient times. The Greeks created sculptures and paintings of the wise goddess and the owl. Greek coins pictured the Little Owl on one side and the face of Athena on the other side.

On the island of Sicily, off the coast of Italy, people dreaded the very sight and sound of an owl. Sicilians believed that if a horned owl sang near a sick person's home for three days, the sick person would die. If the owl sang near a healthy family's home, Sicilians thought someone in the family would develop tonsil pain.

Today, you will find owls in stories, songs, poems, and cartoons.

Cave painting

Ancient Greek coin

Owl sculpture

A scene from the poem "The Owl and the Pussy Cat"

Birds of Prey

Like hawks and eagles, owls are called **raptors,** or **birds of prey,** which means they use sharp talons and curved bills to hunt, kill, and eat other animals.

But owls are different from hawks and eagles in several ways. Most owls have huge heads, stocky bodies, soft feathers, short tails, and a reversible toe that can point either forward or backward. An owl's eyes face forward, like yours do. Most owl species are active at night, not in the daytime.

According to scientists, there are 160 to 175 species of owls in the world. They live on every continent except icy Antarctica.

Owls belong to a group of birds called **Strigiformes** (pronounced STRIG-ih-forms). That group is divided into two smaller groups, known as families. The family called **Tytonidae** (pronounced ty-TON-ih-dee) includes Barn Owls, which have heart-shaped faces. The second family, **Strigidae** (pronounced STRIG-ih-dee), includes all other owls, most of which have round faces.

Barn Owl, with heart-shaped face

Great Horned Owl, with round face

7

rom the Tops of Their Heads . . .

Ears? Horns? No . . . those two bunches of feathers that look like ears are **tufts!** Tufts are specialized feathers that stand up from the heads of many kinds of owls. They have nothing to do with hearing and are much too soft to be horns.

Owls use tufts to help **camouflage,** or disguise, themselves. When the tufts are raised, they resemble small twigs or branches. They help the owls stay hidden from **predators,** animals that hunt other animals. Owls hide from songbirds, too, because the little birds dive and make a racket when they spot an owl, a behavior called **mobbing.** The commotion warns other songbirds that an owl is in the area.

Owls without visible tufts are called **round-headed** owls. Some round-headed owls raise their facial and "eyebrow" feathers to mimic tufts.

Western Screech-Owl
with tufts raised

Northern Saw-whet Owl
with "eyebrow" feathers raised

The Better to Hear You With

Where are those ears anyway? If you looked deep under the head feathers of an owl, you would discover that it has a slit on each side of its skull. Each slit is a flap of skin, called an **ear conch** (pronounced konk), which opens into a large ear canal.

An owl opens and closes its ear conches (pronounced konks) by using muscles beneath the rings of feathers around the owl's face. The rings of feathers are called the **facial disc.** The facial disc captures and funnels sound into the owl's ears, just as a TV satellite dish funnels broadcast signals into its antenna.

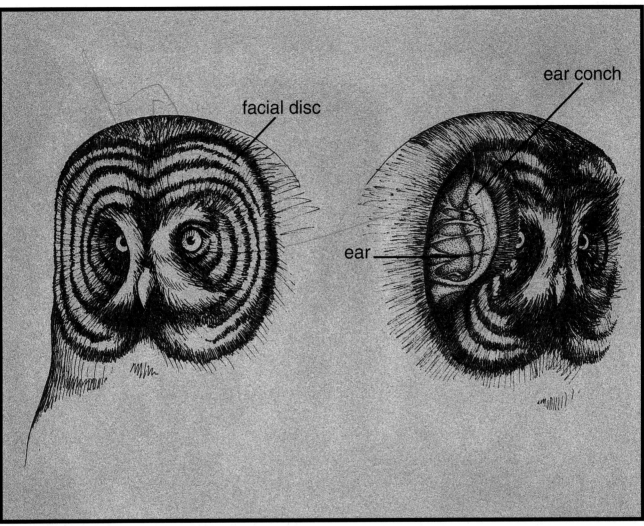

Facial disc and ear conch of a Great Gray Owl

Asymmetrical placement of an owl's ears

skull

higher ear

lower ear

A Boreal Owl locates its prey by sound.

The Eyes Have It

The magnificent eyes of owls come in three colors. Owl species that live in North America have bright yellow or brown eyes. Some European owls have orange eyes.

A thin tissue, called the **iris,** covers the front of the eye and gives the eyeball its color. What color is your iris? At the center of the iris is the dark, round **pupil.** The pupil controls how much light gets into the eye. In the bright glare of a sunny day, the pupil shrinks to block out some of the light. At night, the pupil expands to let in lots of light. An owl's large pupils help it hunt in the dark.

People once thought that owls were blind during the day. Obviously, this is false—the Ferruginous Pygmy-Owl is one of many owl species that hunt in broad daylight.

A Ferruginous Pygmy-Owl
has yellow eyes.

A Barred Owl has brown eyes.

A European Eagle Owl has
orange eyes.

ome owl species have eyes larger than yours! An owl's eyes contain cells that are sensitive to light, just like your eyes do. Named after their shapes, these cells are called **rods** and **cones.**

Rods help you see in dim light. Cones help you see color. An owl's eyes are packed with rods, so the bird sees well in the dark. However, its eyes contain few cones, so what you see in color looks mostly black and white to an owl.

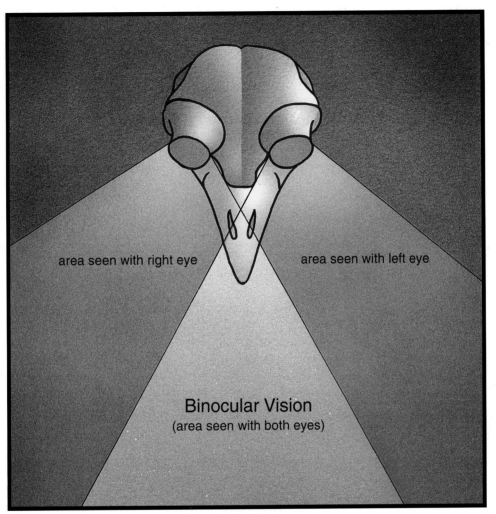

area seen with right eye

area seen with left eye

Binocular Vision
(area seen with both eyes)

An owl's field of vision

have 14 neck bones—that is double the number that you have. These neck bones, along with a special bone at the base of the skull, allow movement. An owl can turn its head 270 degrees in both directions—that is more than halfway around its body, but not quite a full turn around. Unlike you, an owl can swivel its head around to see who might be sneaking up from behind.

19

hen you blink, your eyelids close from above, like window shades, briefly covering your eyes. Figuring out how an owl's eyelids work is not so simple, because owls have three sets of eyelids.

An owl's upper eyelids are like yours. They cover the owl's eyes when it blinks. The lower eyelids rise from below, covering the owl's eyes when it is asleep.

The third set of eyelids, called **nictitating** (pronounced NIK-tih-tay-ting) **membranes,** stretches from the inside corner to the outside corner of each eye. These thin, cloudy membranes close diagonally to cover the eyes. Scientists think that nictitating membranes protect, moisten, and clean the owl's eyes, just as wipers clean the windshield of a car.

**Whiskered Screech-Owl
blinking its upper eyelids**

**Whiskered Screech-Owl
closing its lower eyelids
as it falls asleep**

**Whiskered Screech-Owl using
its nictitating membranes**

hantom Flyers

Have you ever wished that you could fly? Owls fly skillfully without much effort, because their wings are large compared with the size and weight of their bodies. With large wings and a light body, owls can carry heavy prey animals, fly among thick vegetation and trees, and hover above open fields.

Shhh! Sit as silently as possible. Do you suppose you might see an owl fly by? If you sat outside on a moonlit night and were very quiet, you might see an owl fly past, but you probably would not hear it. Thanks to their special feathers, many owls fly almost silently. The outer edges of their forward wing feathers have a stiff fringe, like the teeth of a comb. The rear wing feathers have a soft, hairlike fringe. These fringed edges soften the flow of air as it moves over the wings. The fine, velvety surface of the flight feathers absorbs the noise the feathers make as they slide over one another.

The ability to fly so quietly gives the owl a big advantage. It can hear the scampering of its prey, but the prey animal may not hear the owl approach. The owl may quietly sneak up on and capture the prey.

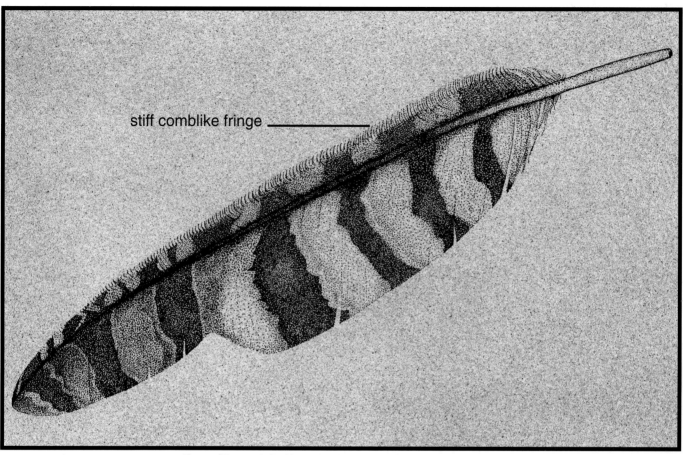

stiff comblike fringe

Great Horned Owl's wing feather with comblike fringe

Fancy Feathers

Many owls look bigger than they really are because they are heavily covered with feathers from top to bottom.

In most species, female and male owls have similar feather colors and markings, but the female is usually larger than the male. Adult owls lose their feathers and grow new ones every year, but each owl stays the same color throughout its life.

However, owls of the same species may be different colors. Eastern Screech-Owls, for example, might be brownish gray or reddish orange. The color of an Eastern Screech-Owl's feathers is determined before it hatches from its egg—in the same way that the color of your hair and eyes is determined before you are born.

Brownish gray (left) and reddish orange (right) Eastern Screech-Owls

he colors of an owl's feathers help it blend in with the natural environment. Body feathers also keep the owl warm, as if it were wrapped in a soft, downy blanket.

Snowy Owls have white feathers that help them hide in their snowy habitat. The hollow shafts of their white feathers hold heat for a long time, helping Snowy Owls stay warm.

The Flammulated Owl's dark feathers blend well with tree bark in the forests where it lives. The feather color helps camouflage the Flammulated Owl when it tucks up against a tree for a nap. Dark feathers warm up quickly in the sunlight. This may help dark-colored owls stay warm when they roost during the day.

Short-eared Owls live in open grasslands or prairies. Their light brown feathers match the tan grasses and the brown earth. Light brown feathers absorb heat from the sun, keeping the Short-eared Owl warm.

If you wanted to hide in a corner of your room, what color of clothing would best camouflage you?

A well-camouflaged Flammulated Owl

eather colors are not the only things that help camouflage owls. They have other neat tricks to **conceal,** or hide, themselves. Many stand tall and pull their feathers in tightly, making the owls skinnier and harder to see. When trying to conceal themselves, owls raise the whitish feathers surrounding the bill. Tufted owls also raise their tufts, and round-headed owls lift their facial and "eyebrow" feathers.

When an owl tries to hide itself by changing its shape, it is in **concealment posture.** In this posture, the owl's rounded outline is broken up and is less likely to be seen by humans or predators.

Long-eared Owl in concealment posture

oes and Talons

You have five toes on each foot. Owls have four toes on each foot. Two toes point forward, one toe points backward, and the "reversible" outer toe of each foot can point either forward or backward as the owl wishes. Sometimes three of the owl's toes point forward, sometimes only two. With two toes pointing forward and two back, the owl can perch securely on a branch. When the owl clutches its prey, its toes spread so the owl can get a firm grip.

At the end of each toe is a long, sharp claw called a **talon.** The owl uses its talons to snatch, squeeze, and kill prey animals. It also uses talons to defend itself against predators, such as hawks, other owls, badgers, and raccoons.

Many owls have feathered legs and feet. Researchers think that these feathers are for warmth. Snowy Owls, which live in the cold Arctic, have heavily feathered legs and feet. Elf Owls, which live in warm, southern climates, have lightly feathered legs.

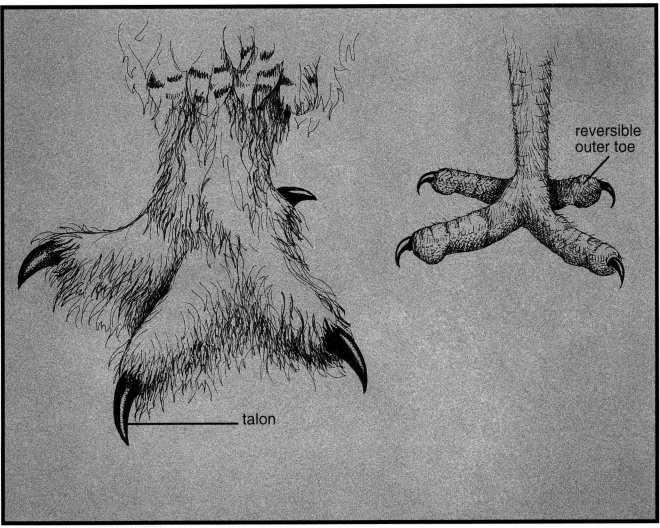

reversible
outer toe

talon

Snowy Owl's heavily feathered leg and foot   **Elf Owl's lightly feathered leg and foot**

A Flammulated Owl feeds on a moth.

Owls hunt in various ways. One hunting technique is called **perch and pounce.** In this method owls perch comfortably until they see their victim, then glide down upon it. Another approach to hunting, called **quartering flight,** is to search for prey while flying. Sometimes owls—most often owls that hunt in open country—**hover** like a helicopter above prey until they are ready to zoom in on it. Hovering takes a lot of energy. Burrowing Owls commonly run across the ground after their prey. In all methods, owls generally hunt close to the ground so that they can more easily hear and see their prey.

A Northern Hawk-Owl perches and prepares to pounce.

A Barn Owl hunts using the quartering flight technique.

A Short-eared Owl hovers in flight while hunting.

A Burrowing Owl hunts prey by running.

wls sometimes hide their food. They capture prey and use their bill to carefully stuff the food into a hiding spot. This is called **caching** (pronounced CASH-ing). Owls might cache prey in holes in trees, in the forks of tree branches, behind rocks, or in clumps of grass. Have you ever cached special toys or treats so that others would not find them? Owls might do this when the hunting is good in order to stock up. Usually, owls go back for the prey within a day or two.

A Northern Pygmy–Owl caches a mouse in a tree hole.

 **anging Out**

At the end of a day or night spent hunting, owls return to a resting place, called a **roost.** This spot is sometimes shared with other owls of the same species. A resting area shared by a group of owls is called a **communal roost.**

Owls may benefit in one or more ways from sharing the same roost. The owls can watch for mobbing songbirds and predators. They may also huddle together to keep each other warm. Shared roosts probably make it easier for owls to find partners during the mating season. Owls may even pass along information about good hunting spots. The roost is commonly located next to good hunting grounds so owls can search for prey as soon as they leave or return to the roost.

Long-eared Owls at a communal roost

Pellet Packing

Remember having the flu and how much you hated throwing up? Imagine throwing up each time that you ate! Owls vomit ten to twenty hours after every meal.

Unlike you, owls swallow their food whole or in large pieces, without chewing it. An owl's stomach doesn't contain the digestive juices needed to break down swallowed fur, feathers, teeth, beaks, bones, insect shells, or other hard body parts. Inside the owl's stomach, these hard pieces are packed into tight, sausage-shaped clumps called **pellets.** Owls usually spit up pellets onto the ground beneath their favorite roosts.

Researchers study pellets to determine what each species of owl eats. Using special tools, they gently tease open the pellets and pick them apart. Sometimes they can re-create the prey animal's skeleton with pieces of bone, like putting together a jigsaw puzzle. The skeleton may turn out to be an animal that was not known to live in the area where the owl hunted, killed, and ate it. In this way, owl pellets help scientists make important discoveries.

Owl pellet, whole and split open

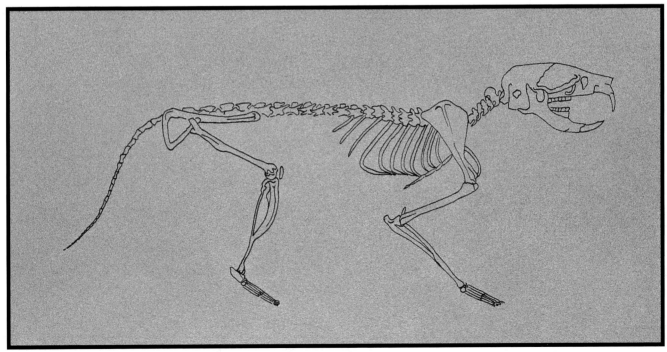

Skeleton of a vole

airing Up

Late winter is mating time for most owls. Males begin seeking mates by calling through the afternoon and evening air.

Generally, the large owls hoot and the small owls toot. The large Barred Owl hoots in a loud, low call that sounds like a question, Who cooks for you? Who cooks for you all? The small Northern Saw-whet Owl sings in a rapid, high tone that some people think sounds like a file being scraped across the teeth of a saw. Toot, toot, toot is the way their singing sounds.

A female owl listens for a call that interests her. She will only respond to calls from males of the same species. Once a male owl gains the interest of a female, he starts performing, or showing off. He might display his feathers by fluffing them out. He might give the female gifts of food. Some males even "sky dance." A male Short-eared Owl will circle high above the female he is courting and clap his wings under his belly several times during a dive. Then he will fly up again and hang in the wind. He may repeat this dance several times, all in an effort to impress the female. At the end of the performance, the male dives past the female into the grass. If the female follows him, the two owls may become a mating pair.

Male Short-eared Owl "sky dancing." The female watches, then follows the male into the grass.

ating owls spend a great deal of time together. They may rub their bills across each other's heads and facial discs. This gesture is called **preening.** Scientists think it reduces fighting and other aggressive behavior. It also helps owls keep their feathers in good condition. Many owl pairs stretch their necks forward toward their mates and coo, as if they enjoy the preening session.

Spotted Owls preening

45

and-Me-Down Homes

Owls are talented hunters, but nest builders they are not. Many owls take advantage of the hard work performed by other animals, instead of building their nests from scratch.

Large owls, like Great Horned Owls, use nests in trees or on cliffs that were built and abandoned by hawks, crows, magpies, or other birds. Many owls simply nest in holes, called **hollows,** in trees. These tree holes occur naturally, or they are pecked into trees by woodpeckers. Elf Owls nest in saguaro cacti, where woodpeckers have created ready-made holes.

Barn Owls typically nest in the rafters of barns, in empty buildings or silos, or on cliffs. Burrowing Owls live up to their name by nesting in underground tunnels that were dug by ground squirrels, prairie dogs, badgers, or other burrowing animals. Some Burrowing Owls use their feet and bills to dig burrows themselves. Snowy Owls and Short-eared Owls build simple nests on the ground.

Scientists think female owls pick out the nest sites. Together, the owl pair defends their nest. The nest area will be the owl family's home for several months.

Stick nest

Natural tree hollow

Woodpecker hole

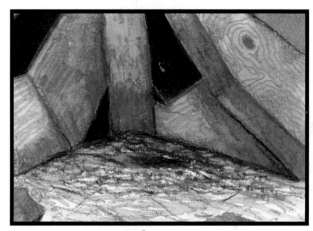

Rafters of a barn

Ground nest

Burrow

Raising a Family

If food supplies are low in a given year, owl pairs may not breed. But if enough food is available to feed a growing family, female owls lay one to fourteen roundish white eggs. Females from different owl species lay different numbers of eggs. The number also depends on how much food is available. For example, if the nearby mouse population is high, a female Short-eared Owl might lay ten eggs. If the mouse population is low, she might lay just four eggs.

Eggs are usually laid one to four days apart. The female owl sits on the eggs to keep them warm. This is called **incubation.** During the incubation period, the female loses the feathers on her belly. She presses the warm bare skin, or **brood patch,** against the eggs.

Brood patch of a female Long-eared Owl

aby owls, called **owlets** or **nestlings**, hatch 22 to 40 days after the eggs are laid. Because eggs are laid on different days, owlets break free from their shells on different days. This is called **asynchronous** (pronounced ay-SIN-kruh-nuhs) **hatching.** The first owlets to hatch can be one to two weeks older than the last ones to hatch.

When young owls hatch, they are covered with white, downy feathers and their eyes are closed. Several days after hatching, their feathers turn gray and their eyes open.

Male owls hunt and bring food to the nest. Female owls tear small pieces of meat off the prey animals and feed them to the nestlings. Owls grow up quickly. In just three or four weeks, the owlets start to eat prey animals whole and spit up pellets.

Nestlings compete with each other for food. Because the older nestlings are bigger and stronger than those born a few days later, they often get most of the meat. If food is scarce, the younger owlets may even starve to death.

When the owlets are two to three weeks old, both parents may leave the nest to hunt. The owlets cry out to their parents for food, just as you did as a baby when you were hungry. These cries are called **food-begging calls.**

Great Gray Owl with nestlings

Short-eared owlets develop faster than any other North American species. They start to venture outside the nest when they are just two weeks old. Barn owlets are the slowest to develop, staying in the nest until they are about eight weeks old.

Owlets raised in tree nests, like Northern Hawk-Owls, climb on nearby branches until they are ready to fly. Owlets raised in ground nests, like Short-eared Owls, wander around on the ground until they can fly. This period of exploration is called **branching** or **nest dispersal.** When owlets first gain the ability to fly, they are called **fledglings.**

By autumn, parents are finished raising their families. The fledglings have grown their adult feathers, and they are now full-sized owls. The young adults are ready for life on their own. Owls may live up to 25 years. Generally, the larger species of owls live longer than the smaller species.

Northern Hawk–Owls branching

The Future of Our Feathered Friends

Young adult owls live where they find the same type of food, water, shelter, and space as where they were raised. The place where an animal naturally lives and grows is called its **habitat.** Forest, grassland, desert, tundra, and wooded gully habitats have plants, landforms, and animals that are important to the survival of each owl species that lives there. For example, Short-eared Owls survive in northern grassland habitat, which has grasses and other plants that hide the owls' roosts and nests. These grasslands are also habitat for the small rodents that Short-eared Owls eat. Southern desert habitat has saguaro cacti that Elf Owls nest in, and the insects, spiders, scorpions, and small reptiles that they eat. Great Horned Owls nest and hunt in almost every natural habitat. What is in your habitat that helps you live and grow?

Sometimes we destroy owl habitat, particularly when we clear land of the plants that naturally grow there. This forces owls to move, and it means that more owls must crowd into less space. The crowded areas may not have the food supply to nourish all the owls sharing the space. Some owls, even the Great Horned Owls, may starve.

You and owls need a healthy habitat in which to live and grow. It is important that we find a balance between our use of land and wildlife's need for habitat. Now that you know WHOO owls are, you will be more able to make wise choices about protecting them and

Great Horned Owl

their habitats. Tell your family and friends the neat things you have learned about owls. Get involved with nature centers in your area—or start a nature club of your own. Most of all, treat wildlife and their habitats with respect.

Thanks for giving a hoot about owls!

lossary: Words for the Wise about Owls

Abandoned. Given up.

Adaptations. Adjustments to environmental conditions, particularly to new or changing conditions.

Asymmetrical. Uneven or unbalanced.

Asynchronous Hatching. Eggs hatching over a number of days in the order in which they were laid.

Binocular Vision. Vision in which both eyes see an overlapping scene.

Birds of Prey or **Raptors.** Birds that use their sharp talons and curved bills to hunt and eat other animals.

Branching or **Nest Dispersal.** The period of time when baby birds first leave the nest to climb on branches or explore the ground near the nest.

Brood Patch. A patch of bare skin on a female owl's belly that forms during the incubation period. She presses the brood patch against her eggs to keep them warm.

Camouflage. To hide by blending in with the surrounding environment.

Carnivores. Animals that survive by eating meat or animal tissue.

Caching. Hiding or storing something, such as food, for later use.

Communal Roost. A resting area shared by a group of birds.

Conceal. The act of hiding to avoid being seen.

Concealment Posture. A temporary change in the form of an animal's body that allows it to conceal itself.

Cone. A cone-shaped cell in the eye that is sensitive to color.

Crepuscular. Active during the early morning and early evening hours.

Diurnal. Active during the day.

Ear Conch. The external opening of an owl's ear.

Environment. One's surroundings.

Facial Disc. The ring of feathers surrounding an owl's face.

Field of Vision. The entire area that can be seen at any instant without moving one's head.

Fledgling. A young bird that has gained the ability to fly.

Food-Begging Calls. Cries for food made by young animals.

Fossils. Preserved impressions, bones, or other remains of ancient life.

Habitat. The place or environment, including food, water, shelter, and space, where a plant or animal naturally lives or grows.

Hollow. A hole in a tree that either occurs naturally or is carved by a woodpecker.

Hover. To hang fluttering in the air.

Incubation. Sitting on eggs to keep them warm.

Insectivores. Animals that eat insects.

Iris. A thin tissue that gives the eyeball its color.

Mobbing. A behavior in which songbirds dive on a predator and make noise, thus warning other songbirds that the predator is near.

Nestling. A young bird that has not yet left the nest.

Nictitating Membranes. A set of thin, cloudy eyelids that close diagonally across an owl's eyes.

Nocturnal. Active during the night.

Owlet. A baby owl.

Pellet. A clump of tightly packed, indigestible materials such as fur, bones, and feathers.

Perch or **Roost.** (verb) To sit and rest or sleep.

Perch and Pounce. A hunting technique in which owls perch until they locate their prey, then pounce upon it.

Population. The number of organisms living in an area.

Preening. A behavior in which one bird grooms the feathers of another bird.

Predator. An animal that hunts, kills, and eats other animals.

Prey. An animal hunted or killed for food by another animal.

Pupil. The dark, round center of the eyeball.

Quartering Flight. A hunting technique in which an owl searches for prey while flying.

Rod. A rod-shaped cell in the eye that is sensitive to light.

Roost. (noun) A place where birds rest.

Round-headed. Without tufts.

Sclerotic Ring. A structure made of 12 to 15 bony plates that holds the front of the eyeball in place.

Species. A group of plants or animals that have certain characteristics in common.

Strigidae. The owl family that includes round-faced owls.

Strigiformes. The order of animals that includes owls.

Symmetrical. Even or balanced.

Talon. The sharp, curved claw of a bird of prey.

Tuft. A cluster of specialized feathers that rises from the top of an owl's head.

Tytonidae. The owl family that includes barn owls.

Index

bout the Authors

★ **Kila Jarvis** teaches third grade in Missoula, Montana. An avid birdwatcher and naturalist, she learned to catch and study owls in the field as a volunteer on owl research projects. From this experience, Jarvis developed a classroom unit that integrates owls into all subject areas.

★ **Denver W. Holt** is a wildlife biologist and president of the Owl Research Institute in Missoula, an internationally recognized center dedicated to the study and conservation of owls and their habitat. Holt has written numerous scientific papers on his studies of owls in Montana, Alaska, and Costa Rica. Holt's work has caught the attention of CNN and magazines and newspapers across the country and around the world.

About the Illustrators

★ **Leslie Leroux**, a wildlife biologist and artist, studied art at the Nova Scotia College for Art and Design and the New York School of Visual Art.

★ **Courtney Couch** is a wildlife artist with a bachelor's degree in wildlife management. She works as a hydrological technician in western Montana.

★ **Ed Jenne,** a professional illustrator for over 16 years and creator of the "owlphabet," likes to draw almost as much as he likes to fly fish.

Authors Kila Jarvis and Denver W. Holt check the flight feathers of a Long-eared Owl.
—Michael Gallacher photo